T0279972

Difficult
Conversations
Don't Have to be
Difficult

a fable about communication

Difficult Conversations
Don't Have to be
Difficult

**A SIMPLE, SMART WAY TO
MAKE YOUR RELATIONSHIPS
AND TEAM BETTER**

Jon
GORDON
Bestselling author of
The Energy Bus

Amy P.
KELLY
Bestselling Co-Author of
The Energy Bus Field Guide

WILEY

Published by John Wiley & Sons, Inc., Hoboken, New Jersey.
Published simultaneously in Canada.

For general information on our other products and services or for technical support, please contact our Customer Care Department within the United States at (800) 762-2974, outside the United States at (317) 572-3993 or fax (317) 572-4002.

Wiley also publishes its books in a variety of electronic formats. Some content that appears in print may not be available in electronic formats. For more information about Wiley products, visit our web site at www.wiley.com.

Library of Congress Cataloging-in-Publication Data is Available

ISBN 9781394187171 (cloth)
ISBN 9781394187188 (ePub)
ISBN 9781394187195 (ePDF)

Cover Design: Paul McCarthy

SKY10074208_043024

We dedicate this book to our families and all the business professionals, athletes, teachers, medical professionals, family members, administrators, and anyone who has ever cared enough to have the difficult conversations. May those conversations be less challenging and your relationships and teams stronger and more unified after reading this book.

—Jon and Amy

Contents

	Acknowledgments	*ix*
	Introduction	*xi*
1	**Turmoil**	**1**
2	**Transparency**	**11**
3	**Truth**	**17**
4	**Tiles of Talent: Embracing Hybrid Team Trust**	**31**
5	**Trust**	**47**
6	**Time to Transform**	**69**
7	**Team**	**73**
8	**Application of the STAR³ Model**	**81**
	Difficult Conversations Don't Have to be Difficult *Resources*	*87*
	About the Authors	*89*
	Other Books by Jon Gordon	*91*

Acknowledgments

We want to acknowledge our families, especially our spouses and children and extended family, who've been a part of many challenging conversations to grow stronger together.

We want to acknowledge our Jon Gordon Team of speakers, trainers, and consultants. This group has worked diligently to provide personal and professional development to the individuals and teams we serve while practicing what we believe in. It is the commitment to our relationships that we want to acknowledge and for which we express deep gratitude as we continue to serve together in our shared vision and greater purpose.

Thank you for getting better together and living these truths: The Team Is the Star, and No One Creates Success Alone!

Introduction

Jon and I have worked together for eight years and the idea for this book came about because of a difficult conversation we were having. We figured if our team was struggling with having these types of conversations that were necessary for growth, then other teams were likely struggling as well. We'd seen this time and again in our work and felt it was an impactful area to go deeper.

We thought about all the best practices we have learned and shared working with many of the best corporate, school, and sports teams on the planet. We decided to create a model for teams to have conversations and discussions they needed to have but were avoiding because of fear of conflict or fear of having conflict ruin the team.

Our brainstorming sessions led to us creating the STAR^3 model and we immediately began sharing it with our clients and audiences. The response was incredible.

We discovered that one of the primary characteristics of the most successful teams and organizations is that they don't just celebrate the positive aspects of success; they also address the inevitable negativity, challenges, and disagreements that come up in life and work. They have the difficult conversations but in a positive way. We witnessed this firsthand and saw how this created stronger bonds, greater cohesiveness, and unity. We've seen transformations that are not only profitable but deeply impactful on a personal level in the lives of the people involved.

Many people agree with the concept of addressing disagreements and negativity, but many struggle with how to do this in a constructive way.

We wrote this book to prepare the way for greater effectiveness for you and your team. We look forward to all that you will accomplish together through the strength and effectiveness of your conversations.

As you will read, the STAR^3 model provides a framework to elevate the results of your most challenging conversations to unify your teams and strengthen each individual's communication and leadership in the process.

We hope you enjoy the book and utilize the STAR^3 model for a simple, smart way to improve your relationships and team.

—Jon and Amy
JonGordon.com

Chapter 1

Turmoil

The Calendar

Ruth looked at her calendar and groaned. What she saw made her head pound and her stomach clench. Her laptop screen was covered in colors representing meetings from early morning to late at night. The packed days of back-to-back meetings extended weeks into the future. Ruth knew she could not keep up this pace and wondered why all her hard work was not producing the results needed to sell her company. Why was her team not able to accomplish the goals to do the things that would take BBDI, Inc. to the next level and allow her to take a much-needed break?

Ruth had started Breaking Boundaries Data Innovation (BBDI) eight years earlier and built it into a multimillion-dollar enterprise serving a global audience. The shared vision and mission of the organization was to create a world that relies on truth to make better decisions. The foundation of the company's data innovation solutions was software Ruth designed herself. She was proud of the partnerships she created to accelerate the company's growth and her clients' growth. Now she needed her executive team to step up if they were going to accomplish the objectives set by the board of directors.

Ruth shuddered as she stared at her packed calendar. Time is a strange thing, she thought. When you are starting your company and trying to find clients, time moves sufferingly slow as you think about all the ways the business can change the world and also the ways it might fail. But after years of hard work creating a successful company, when it's finally time to sell and reap your reward, there doesn't seem to be enough time in the day to do what matters most.

Her number-one priority right now was to figure out what was wrong with her executive team. The team was not working well together, and Ruth was overwhelmed by the aggressive goals and timeline the board had set for her company. She had chosen every board member and picked long-time professional friends and colleagues who would hold her accountable and challenge her to take her leadership and vision to the next level, but in this case she felt they were taking the accountability thing to an unrealistic level and were hurting her more than helping her. She had great relationships with each board member but when they met collectively the dynamic seemed to change. Personal relationships gave way to ego and power trips where board members jockeyed for who could challenge her the most and take credit for the sale of the company. After all, it would look great on their bios to be a board member of a company that everyone in the industry followed and sold for a huge financial gain. She had heard many stories in the past about boards who abused their power and even removed the company's founder, but she couldn't believe this was even a possibility for her. Yet with boards and business you just never know, she thought, and she was more stressed than ever.

This company was her fifth baby, in addition to her four children at home. She had built it with years of sweat, grit, and hard work, and was determined to finish strong and create a successful exit. Ruth certainly cared more about her company than her board did but she couldn't put her finger on what was wrong with her team. Things were simply not working, and she was desperate to figure out how to get her team to perform at the level necessary to release their new product offering that would allow BBDI to assume a place of dominance in the market, while carving out an entirely new category for business decision management software (BDM). Just like Robert and Kate Kestnbaum were pioneers of database marketing in the 1980s, leading to the rise of the CRM, Ruth and her team would redefine business decision management with a proprietary combination of data innovation solutions and powerful database management. But they had to get a working product out in time before anyone else hit the market and took away their competitive advantage.

Ruth inhaled deeply and exhaled. She shrugged her shoulders as an attempt to loosen up her body the way she did years ago during pressure-filled moments of her college volleyball games. It was time for her weekly executive team meeting, and she needed to clear her mind and focus. She closed her laptop, picked up her leather-bound journal with her notes for the meeting, and started to walk down the hall to the conference room. Her executive meeting began every Wednesday morning at 7:30 a.m. She expected each member of the team to be there and be ready to begin on time. She could see a few faces through the glass door of the conference room as she walked down the hall and was looking for one person in particular but didn't see her. Was Paula there? And if not, how many of the team decided to take the easy way out by logging in online instead of participating in person? The way Paula had been acting lately, Ruth doubted she would see Paula sitting in the conference room.

Paula was the president of BBDI, Inc. She was a powerhouse business strategist and a true thought leader in the data innovation marketspace. Ruth depended on Paula to help drive the organization's operations, product launches, sales, and strategic business objectives, as well as the people on the executive leadership team. But Paula had been acting strange lately. Ruth didn't want to seem paranoid, but she had started to pick up on some disengagement signs from Paula over the past few months. Paula normally did not contradict Ruth's decisions in front of the executive team but lately this had become the norm. When Ruth asked Paula if anything was wrong, she always responded, "Everything is fine." Somehow Ruth didn't believe her.

Ruth opened the glass door to the conference room and scanned the faces at the table. She saw everyone she expected to see either in the room or online. The only face she did not see was Paula's. No one in the group was talking. People were looking at their laptop screens, drinking coffee, tea, or energy drinks, and waiting for her to start the meeting. At least everyone had their cameras turned on. Ruth's executive assistant, John, looked at her and mouthed that he had texted Paula to see if she was having technical issues but had not heard anything back yet.

Ruth smiled at John and calmly said good morning. She chose not to say anything about Paula's absence and sat down at the head of the table while checking the time on her phone. It was 7:26 a.m.. Ruth filled the awkward silence by asking a few of the team members how their day was going, but she didn't hear a word they said because thoughts of Paula's absence were filling her mind, frustrating her.

Time inched forward to 7:30 a.m., and Ruth knew she needed to start the meeting. However, with everything that was happening with the new product launch, she did not want the president to miss the important discussion topics. The fact that Paula was not setting a good example for the team frustrated Ruth. This was a time when the group needed to raise their level of commitment, not drop their standards of excellence.

As the time turned to 7:32 a.m., Ruth let out a sigh of disappointment and started the meeting.

The Meeting

Ruth welcomed the team and began the meeting by asking for their updates. Each leader shared the progress on their objectives. Ruth listened and made notes. None of the team asked questions or talked about how their work impacted each leader's teams cross-functionally. No one talked about any challenges they were facing. Everyone focused on their own responsibilities, but there was no discussion about how their progress or lack thereof impacted their overall goals and team success—just one-sided updates, in which the team was just checking the boxes to get the meeting completed so they could get on with their day.

After the VP of HR finished presenting, Paula's voice came through the conference room line before the next person could start. She apologized for being late and, off camera, said she would share her update last.

The meeting continued, but Ruth's frustration was growing. She did not understand why Paula would be late and appear to be disengaged from the meeting. She wrote a note to connect with Paula privately later in the day and continued listening to her team. As she looked around the conference room table, it seemed that the group's eyes were glazed over. "Where did the spark in this team go?" she thought to herself. "Why does it feel like there is no passion or purpose in them?"

When the meeting ended, Ruth felt like she wanted to cry. She was a strong woman, but lately that strength was being tested, and she felt her confidence waver. The company she created was crumbling instead of growing stronger, and she felt powerless to do anything about it. Her team no longer cared about their work or each other, and it couldn't be happening at a worse time. Ruth shook her head. "Why are they abandoning me to do this on my own?" she thought.

Difficult Conversations Don't Have to be Difficult

The Elevator

After completing her morning meetings, as Ruth was leaving for lunch she stood in front of the elevator thinking about her frustrating team meeting and her apathetic team. Thankfully her noon meeting was canceled, or she would have been sitting at her desk working through lunch as usual. She was deep in thought when the elevator doors opened and she came face to face with Paula. They stood staring at each other for a moment. Even though Paula looked like her usual self, her energy was different. Ruth tried to make eye contact but Paula wouldn't look her in the eyes. Ruth asked if she had time for lunch. Paula smiled politely and declined as she whisked past Ruth with a promise to connect later in the day.

Ruth got on the elevator and watched Paula turn into Mitch's office before the elevator doors closed. Mitch was the Vice President of Operations, and his team was behind on their deliverables for the new product launch. Ruth hoped Paula was headed to his office to offer guidance and support. She would make sure to ask Paula about Mitch when they connected later in the day.

Chapter 2

Transparency

The First Surprise

Ruth sat at her desk and waited for Paula. She had booked the only time she saw available on Paula's calendar and was getting frustrated that Paula was not on time for their 5 p.m. meeting. When the clock said 5:05 p.m., she sighed and got up to see if Paula was still in her office. Just as Ruth started to get up to find Paula, she entered the doorway. Paula apologized for her delay and closed the door to Ruth's office before sitting down in one of the chairs across from Ruth's desk.

Ruth thought that was a little strange. Paula did not normally close the door, but perhaps she had something confidential to discuss, which was not surprising considering all the product launch planning that was happening. The BBDI team did not want the competition to get wind of the new product information or the timing of when it was officially coming to market. Maybe that required a closed-door meeting.

As Ruth waited for Paula to get settled, she noticed that Paula was wearing different clothing than earlier in the day. When she got off the elevator, she had been wearing a navy pantsuit and now was wearing jeans and a hoodie with the company logo. Ruth looked at Paula and prepared to have a difficult conversation about how distracted she seemed. Ruth knew it was going to be difficult to tell Paula how she was dropping the ball, but it had to be done.

Paula started speaking before Ruth could say anything. She said, "Ruth, this isn't easy for me to say, but I wanted to let you know as soon as possible and in person. I am resigning from BBDI, and my last day will be two weeks from next Monday."

Ruth was stunned. She knew something was off with Paula's behavior, but she did not expect this. She said, "I'm surprised and sorry to hear this. Can you tell me why?"

Paula looked at Ruth and shook her head slightly. The two had been working together for over seven years and had supported each other through many personal and professional ups and downs.

Paula said, "My son has been sick for over six months, and you don't even know. You've been so focused on selling the company that we haven't been communicating. You haven't had any time for me. I kept waiting for it to change, but it's gotten progressively worse. Every time I tried to talk to you, all you did was talk about the product launch and your own feelings and your own family and business struggles but you refused to listen to me. I'm very grateful for all you've taught me over the years and the opportunities you've extended, so I want this to be a professional ending. It's become obvious that you don't seem to care about me or the team anymore. You don't give us any flexibility, and I have to be in the office all the time. We cannot do our best work in an environment where there is a lack of trust, especially within the leadership of this company. Other people see it throughout the company. It's damaging our culture and our morale."

Paula paused and started again. "I shouldn't speak for anyone else. I take that last part back. Just know that it's not easy for me to leave, but I do not feel we are working as a team anymore. It feels like it's all about you and the sale. I want to move on while we can still remember the good times. I need to take care of my son, and you know that I will always wish you well."

Ruth didn't know what to say. She felt a little blindsided, and she tried to parse the statements coming from Paula. She valued both her professional and her personal relationships with Paula and did not want to cause any further damage. She knew she needed to think before discussing this further. "Why is Paula doing this to me now," she wondered, "after all I've done for her?" But Ruth managed to keep that thought to herself.

She said, "I realize you've been thinking about this, and I want to talk to you a bit more before we do anything else. Could you give me the evening to organize my thoughts, and we can revisit our conversation tomorrow afternoon? You are important to me, your family is important to me, and I want to have some time before we finish this conversation, if possible."

Paula took a breath and replied, "Yes, we can meet to finish this conversation tomorrow. I understand you want to think about what I shared, but I also want you to know that you cannot change my mind. This has been coming for a while. Every day it kept going further in the wrong direction. We can continue the conversation tomorrow, but I still want to plan for my two weeks' notice to start next Monday. Until we talk tomorrow, I do not plan to say anything to anyone else. I'll see you then."

Paula got up and headed to the door. She turned around in the doorway. Ruth took the opportunity to say, "Thank you for giving me some time to digest what you shared. I appreciate it, Paula. You mean a great deal to me and the company. Just like you, I want our relationship to stay positive. I'll see you tomorrow." She did care about Paula, but inside she kept asking herself how Paula could do this to her. Of course, she had been focused on the product launch lately. Ruth also had a lot to balance with her husband and four children at home. She and Paula had worked the last seven years together to get to this point, and truth be told it was the most important thing in her life right now. This wasn't a time to abandon ship but rather to suck it up and push through it.

Ruth looked down at her hands, which were shaking. The movement was strong enough to make her laptop move a bit on her desk, blurring all the meetings on her calendar into an image that looked like a colorful pot of boiling water.

Chapter 3

Truth

The Parking Garage

Ruth rode the elevator to the parking garage. She had tried to focus on her work after the meeting with Paula but just could not bring herself to answer the emails from the rest of the team and the board with all the thoughts about Paula swirling in her head.

How would she explain her president leaving right before the new product launch?

What would the other team members think of her leadership?

What would this do to her reputation with the board?

She wanted to minimize the damage and protect herself. She knew that changes would need to happen. Ruth did not know all the steps she would need to take, but one of the things she would do immediately was to mandate that all the executive leaders work from the office. No more remote work—that had to stop. She had long thought that this was one of the primary factors causing the team's performance to lag, and she was going to put a stop to that quickly. She needed to see everyone working in the office to know that they were actually doing the things that needed to be done for the company's success.

Ruth walked through the parking garage toward her car and clicked her key fob to unlock the doors. The usual chirp that signified the doors unlocking did not occur. She pressed the button on the fob again. Again, nothing happened. She walked up next to the door and tried one more time. Still nothing.

Ruth was wondering what to do next when a small vehicle pulled up behind her. There was a rotating yellow light on top of the vehicle, and a sign on the side reading "Security." A smiling face peered out of the window at Ruth.

"Can I help you?" asked the face in the window.

Ruth turned to the car and said, "I'm trying to get into my car to drive home, but it appears my key fob won't work."

"That's frustrating. Let me see what I can do to help you."

The woman in the small vehicle got out and walked next to Ruth. She stuck out her hand and said, "My name is Teresa, but you can call me "T." My job is to keep everyone in the building safe."

Ruth said, "I really appreciate your help. Hopefully it's nothing too serious."

T asked if she could see Ruth's key fob and tried the button to unlock the door one more time. Nothing. Then she said, "I've seen this before. Sometimes when the car battery is dead, everything stops responding. We can check the batteries in your key fob, and we can check the battery in your car. I bet one of them will be the culprit."

T walked to the front of the car to look under the hood. She asked Ruth to press the button on the side of the key fob to extract the manual key option for the car. Ruth understood what T was asking her to do and chided herself for not remembering that feature. Her thinking was so jumbled with all that was going on with the company and the team that even the smallest tasks were challenging.

Her volleyball coach in college had told her that mental clutter creates chaos in her thinking and undermines effective execution, and her clutter and chaos were at an all-time high. *Breathe*, she told herself while she inhaled and exhaled deeply.

Ruth managed to open the door with the manual key and tried to start the car with the ignition button, but nothing happened. She pressed the button on the dashboard to pop the hood of the car so T could take a look. In the rearview mirror, Ruth saw T removing some cables from her security vehicle. She then walked toward the hood of Ruth's car and affixed the cables to the battery.

"Just what I thought," said T. "Your battery is dead. We can probably jump it, but you're going to need to get a new one. This one looks like it's done for."

Ruth was wondering how she could tell the battery was dead just by looking at it but she was so tired she didn't really care.

"Thank you, T. Can you help me jump this one, so I can get home and figure out how to get the battery replaced?"

"Of course I can. I'm here to help. It's what I love about this job. People think I just drive around in my little security vehicle trying to catch people doing things wrong. But I love helping when things go wrong so we can make things right. I know you and the rest of the workers at BBDI have been working around the clock for months, and you have a lot on your plate with the new product launch."

Ruth was shocked to hear T mention the product launch. That was confidential information, but she was just grateful to have someone help her get her car started.

T got the cables hooked up to Ruth's car and connected to the security vehicle. After they turned on the vehicles, they waited for the battery in Ruth's car to charge.

Ruth took another deep breath, got out of her car, and walked over to T's car to say thank you. She asked T, "How long have you been working here?"

T replied, "I've been here for ten years. I was here when you and the team moved into the building about six years ago. I remember being excited to have all the floors in the building occupied."

Ruth was surprised they had never met before, but before she could say anything, T said, "I've enjoyed watching you grow your team and your business, Ruth. It's been an honor to keep you all safe."

Ruth started to feel a little awkward that she did not know more about T and her work in the building. She must be doing a fantastic job, because Ruth had never been aware of any security or safety issues.

T said, "We should probably let the battery charge for a few minutes. While we wait, we can sit on one of the benches by the elevator."

Ruth did not want to delay any longer, but she also trusted that T knew what she was doing, so she complied and followed her to the bench.

The Bench

T sat down and motioned for Ruth to sit next to her on the metal bench near the elevator doors.

Ruth had never sat down in the parking garage before. She could see the setting sun sharing its final rays of light between the concrete levels of the garage. Surprisingly, she felt an unfamiliar stillness and peace, and found herself questioning why she had never noticed the beautiful view of the sky from this spot before. Ruth parked in the same reserved spot every day. She guessed it was because she was always distracted by the things she needed to get done for the business. Her mind was always racing as she entered the office in the mornings, and she was even more distracted at night when she left the building.

T asked Ruth, "How is everything going with you and the team?"

Ruth was not sure she wanted to share the turmoil happening with the resignation of the president of her company but decided T must know how to keep a secret with how well she protected the building and team over the years.

"Well, things have not been going well for a while, but today it all got worse. My president resigned, and I did not see it coming. I haven't been able to get the executive team to come together and perform at the level I know they can, and they all seem more distant all the time."

"Paula resigned? Wow. I can't say I'm surprised, though, with all that's going on with her son and the

Truth

long hours required to lead the team through the product launch," said T.

Ruth was stunned for the second time this evening. "How did you know about Paula's son?"

"I talk to Paula and the team whenever I can. I like to see how everyone is doing, especially when I can tell they have something on their mind. I like to listen to them and see if I can help in some small way," T explained.

"I can help you, too, if you want. No judgment meant by this, but you normally don't seem to see me when you come in and out of the building. I know things are very hectic and demanding and I didn't want to pry. Now is a good time to ask you something I've wanted to ask for a long time. Would you like me to help you, Ruth?" inquired T.

Ruth was not sure what was happening. Was the parking garage security professional trying to coach her in leading her company and executive team? Who was next to offer her advice, the building janitor? Or perhaps the mechanic installing her new battery would also help her with the purchase of her company, she thought sarcastically. Suddenly she felt like she was living in one of the business fables she had read as she climbed the corporate ladder of success. They were encouraging and inspiring and helped her through difficult times and situations, but this was real life and, at this time, she didn't feel like she needed coaching from a security guard.

She turned to T and said, "I appreciate your offer, but I really need to get home and figure out some things.

Let's check on the battery so I can hopefully get out of here." Ruth stood up and walked toward her car.

After T unplugged the cables, Ruth thanked her for all her help, raced out of the parking garage, and sped home to an uncertain future.

The Reckoning

That night as Ruth sat on the couch drinking a glass of wine while her husband and kids were asleep, she thought about T and how kind she was to help her, and the words "I can help you, too, if you want" lingered in her mind. Maybe she had something to say that could help. Ruth's mother always told her that everyone is a teacher, and if you're willing to learn from everyone, they will teach you something valuable. Had she become so cynical and hardened that she thought T had nothing of value to offer her?

Was pride keeping her from success and leading to a fall? She didn't really have to rush out of there. She could have taken just five minutes to listen to T. She knew better than to think she knew everything. After all, T had been talking with many of Ruth's team and they trusted her, so clearly she was someone worth talking to.

Ruth was tired of being tired and sick of the turmoil. Nothing she was doing was working, so perhaps *she* was the problem. Ruth got up and walked to the bathroom, shut the door, and looked at herself in the mirror. *Where have you gone, humble warrior? Why are you thinking only about yourself?*

She began to cry and desperately spoke out loud to the image in the mirror. "What do I do? I don't know what to do!" She knew she needed to try something new and could use all the help she could get. In that moment something shifted, as her pride relented and her need for control faded away. She was open and willing to listen to anyone. She wanted to get better. She needed to get better. She did care about other people, but somewhere along the way she started focusing only on herself. Why couldn't T help her?

She decided she would go see T in the garage before heading to the office in the morning and tell her she was open to hearing her ideas and would receive any help she could provide. She walked to the kitchen, took a frozen breakfast casserole out of the freezer, and put it in the refrigerator so her husband and kids would have break-fast in the morning. She knew she would be out the door before they got up and wanted to show the family love and contribute in some helpful way. She and her husband made a great team, but Ruth knew she had not been engaged enough at home as the pressure increased.

"My goodness," she thought, "am I doing well for anyone in my life right now?" It all led back to the same thing—she needed to try something different and was truly ready for whatever T had to say. She walked back to the couch, laid down, and fell asleep with her clothes on.

The next morning Ruth took a rideshare to work while the auto shop put a new battery in her car. Ruth walked into the garage and found T kneeling by a car and writing down the license plate number. "What are you doing there?" asked Ruth.

"It's a new car I haven't seen before," said T. "Just making sure everything checks out. Keeping you all safe is my number-one priority."

"I appreciate that," said Ruth. "I was wondering if we can finish our conversation from yesterday. I know I rushed out of here, and I wish I had stayed to listen to you after you offered to help."

"That's perfectly fine," said T. "I knew you were distracted and stressed. I'm glad you came to see me this morning. Let's go sit on the bench so we can talk."

Speaking the Truth in Love

T turned to look directly into Ruth's eyes and said, "I've got to be transparent with you, Ruth. I think you've made some mistakes in the last few months, and we have to start with the truth. Keep in mind, I am being transparent with you, because I care. You know what *transparent* means, right? It means to allow light to pass through something so objects behind can be distinctly seen. I want you to know the truth, so you can see what is behind the issues with your team and you can truly move forward together."

Ruth was dumbfounded that a security guard seemed to know more about her team than she did. But though she had a hard time believing it, she reminded herself to be open and humble and listen to what T had to say. She wanted to move forward with her team and get on the right track, and clearly she didn't have the answer at this moment. Ruth responded, "Okay. I can handle it. Tell me what I need to see that I am not seeing now."

T leaned in a little closer and took one of Ruth's hands in hers. She said, "Your ego has become bigger than the mission at BBDI. You are putting yourself and your goals ahead of the team, and maybe even your personal life and family. Your fear is driving you to be self-focused instead of team-focused."

Ruth looked at T. She was a little taken aback by what she was saying. How did T know if Ruth had a big ego or a small ego? How did she know fear was driving her? How did she know anything about her family? All Ruth had ever tried to do was build a company leveraging the best data innovation solutions for the world to make good decisions relying on truth.

As she was thinking about this Ruth felt a little tug in her gut.

She might have started out with a shared vision and mission for how data innovation driving the truth could fuel quality business decisions, but lately all she wanted was to achieve the goals the board set and sell the business at the highest possible price. She was mostly focused on how the sale would make her a success in the eyes of the board, and the sale price would allow her to slow down, take a much-needed break, and reconnect with her family and friends. She had put her life on pause until she achieved her business goals and wanted everyone else to do the same. Ruth wanted certain members of the team always to be in the office, so she could see everything everyone was doing. She needed proof they were working hard. She couldn't remember the last time she really sat down and listened to any of them or said yes to a request for more flexibility in their work. In fact, she regularly vocalized her distrust of people's productivity while working at home, even though many of her team told her it would improve their work–life balance.

One of the most impactful people in her life was her college volleyball coach, and he had always told her and the team that ego disconnects you from others. She certainly didn't feel connected to her team, and it was obvious they didn't feel connected to her. Maybe her ego was getting in the way. Maybe her team felt she didn't care about them anymore. If Paula felt that way, it's likely the rest of the team did, too.

As she was thinking, T continued, "Like I said, I'm telling you this to help you see the issue clearly so you can create solutions for the team and your company. It takes courage to be transparent and tell the truth, and it only works if it is done in love. I mean the type of love that comes with respect and genuine care. While I had never met you before yesterday, I have always assumed the best about you. Even as I saw your team grow more frustrated as they left the building and even more anxious as they walked in, I had a feeling we would talk at some point and you would figure things out and turn things around. I'm glad we finally found ourselves in this moment with time to talk. Now we can take the first step and do what I like to do to help people be bold and brave and have the conversations they need to have to get to the next level. We will create what I call rules of engagement. Rules of engagement include what you can expect from me and what I can expect from you. It helps us approach each other when we need to have the more challenging conversations about important topics that mean a lot to both of us."

Chapter 4

Tiles of Talent: Embracing Hybrid Team Trust

"I really appreciate you sharing this with me, T. I am so sorry we haven't had a chance to speak earlier. I respect the fact that you care enough to tell me the truth, and while you were talking, I remembered something my mentor told me years ago. He always used to say relationships are what matter most. Somehow, I got off course with the busyness and stress of the past months. The pressure from the board and my need to prove my worth and value have been my top priority. I might have even been dealing with impostor syndrome. I can feel like maybe I'm not good enough to really make this company sale happen. In fact, you're probably right. My focus has been on myself, not on what's best for the team or anyone else, really— not the board, not my family, not the rest of the people in the company."

Ruth took a deep breath and continued. "I didn't see it before but now I do. I'm going to get back on track. I'm going to look for ways to build trust back with the team and start by allowing more flexibility in where they do their work, like they've asked me for so many times. I need to tell myself to look at the group as tiles of talent on the screen when we work as a hybrid team instead of telling myself that no one gets as much work done when they're out of the office. Each rectangle on the computer screen represents a unique, valuable, and talented member of our team. I should no longer assume they are less engaged when they are working outside the office. If I want them to trust me, I need to lead the way and build trust."

Tiles of Talent: Embracing Hybrid Team Trust

Ruth continued, "There are quite a few trust builders I can implement, because I know it is not as simple as just providing a more flexible work environment. It is really about the trust, and that takes time and can be different from person to person. Whether it is team members, family members, or board members, if you don't make time for people, they do not believe they matter. Group meetings are not enough. I can't cancel my one-on-one time with the team and expect them to feel valued and important. So, I will also spend time with each person in a one-on-one setting to listen to their concerns instead of always focusing on my own. I know what I need to do, and now I just need to do it. I can't believe I lost sight of what matters most and what I know is key to building a team. I was focused on what's urgent instead of what matters."

T looked at her watch. "That's a great start, Ruth. I'm glad you'll be headed in a new direction, and I know the team will be very happy and benefit. You'll recharge them like we did your battery. But you won't be able to replace them like you did your battery. Because you have the team you have, you need to make them the best they can be."

Ruth looked at T. She could see the sunlight coming through the concrete levels of the parking garage. It had been very cloudy the last week but seeing the sun shining once again gave her a sense of hope for the first time in months.

Ruth thanked T. She knew that just saying thank you wasn't enough for all she had done for her this morning, but it was a start.

As Ruth got in the elevator T said, "You are welcome, Ruth. In addition to what your mentor told you, remember one more thing; it is a fundamental truth my mentor taught me. No one creates success alone. We all need a team to be successful. Just look at you and me. If you add my name to yours, you get confirmation. T + RUTH = TRUTH. Keep that top of mind in the coming days because I believe you are going to need to have some more conversations with your team. Just remember, difficult conversations don't have to be difficult. They are important and required for growth. I'll explain more the next time we talk."

The Second Surprise

When Ruth entered her office, she found the Vice President of Operations, Mitch, standing right inside her door.

Ruth said good morning to Mitch and motioned him to take a seat across from her. He did not normally wait in her office, but this didn't bother Ruth. She just found it odd.

As she sat down, she said, "Good morning, Mitch. How are you doing?"

She noticed Mitch had closed the door before taking a seat.

"I was trying to connect with you yesterday, but your calendar was full, as usual. I'm really sorry to have to deliver this news. I'm resigning my position with BBDI. This has not been an easy decision. I am giving two full weeks' notice, and I will make myself available for one week after that. I am doing everything I can to put you and the team in the best position for the new product launch, even though I will not be a part of it," said Mitch.

Ruth looked at Mitch. She couldn't believe this was happening and hoped he would say, "Never mind, forget what I said. I'm not going anywhere," but he didn't and kept looking back at her earnestly. He did not seem particularly happy or sad. He did seem to feel bad sharing this news, but he also seemed firm in his words.

"May I ask why you're leaving, and why now?" Ruth asked.

"I wanted to talk to you last month, but you had the board meeting to prepare for. I tried to get on your calendar, but I couldn't find the right time. We used to meet at least once a quarter to catch up individually, but there just hasn't been any time with the product launch planning and the pressures and goals you and the board have. You canceled all our one-on-one meetings. I have also been trying to balance my home life with the demands at work. Two months ago, my wife told me that if I did not make her and the kids a priority, she was going to leave me. She said that I've been an absentee father and husband for the last two years. She's brought it up before, but this time I could tell I needed to listen. What we are doing here at BBDI is important, but it is not more important than my family. Especially now that you are honestly more focused on the sale and not as much on our team and the mission we've been on for years. I'm sorry to say that, but you have not noticed the pain this team has been going through for some time."

"Is everyone leaving me?" Ruth mumbled under her breath.

"I'm sorry. I didn't catch what you said," Mitch said softly.

"Nothing. I was just thinking out loud, because I'm a bit surprised for the second time in 48 hours," Ruth replied.

She looked down at her hands. They were shaking again. The meeting colors on her laptop screen were swirling and jumping again.

"Mitch, I appreciate you speaking with me and would like the opportunity to change your mind," said Ruth.

"Ruth, this has been going in the wrong direction for a while, and I must change course to protect my marriage and my family, not to mention my health. I am formally giving my two weeks' notice and will do all I can to help maintain the success of the new product launch. We can talk about how to tell the team and our clients tomorrow. I have the product launch deadlines to manage today, so let's set up another time to discuss the communications about my departure."

"Okay, Mitch. I'll get something on our calendars, but please keep this confidential until then," said Ruth.

"Do not worry. You can trust me," responded Mitch.

The Ego

Ruth sat at her desk. She turned her chair around and looked out the window at the clouds in the sky. She was thinking about the hope she had in the parking garage before coming into the office and now it felt like that hope was being suctioned out of her one conversation and resignation at a time.

What had happened?

She was not ready for another surprise, and yet here it was.

Had she really put herself and her goals ahead of the team and her family and her team's families? Had she forgotten about their lives and their priorities because of her own ambition to sell the company, appease the board, and close an impressive deal? Speaking of the board, with two key resignations on her leadership team before their biggest product launch, she wondered what they would think of her leadership. Would they ask her to resign, or would they just fire her? They would certainly lose confidence in her if she could not fix the problems with the team. First, she knew she needed to find confidence in herself to try something new.

As Ruth looked out the window, she replayed her conversation with T.

She realized that her battery being dead was a blessing in disguise because she was way off course and needed a new path forward. If she could keep Paula and Mitch from leaving and engage her team more, she could turn things around. It wasn't too late if she could keep her team intact.

Ruth took a moment and started writing in her leather journal the things T shared. She knew she would need them for the conversation she had scheduled with Paula later that day.

After Ruth recorded all the elements of the conversation in her journal, she looked at the page. She noticed that the different points spelled out *STARRR*—the word *STAR* with three *R*s.

This is interesting, thought Ruth. T's advice was shining like a star off her journal page. It rekindled her hope as she looked intently at her notes.

The *S* stood for "Small Ego, Big Mission." It was about WE > ME. She had allowed the Me to come before the WE (her team), and now she was experiencing the consequences. Change had to start with her and that would be the first thing she would address when she talked with Paula. Speaking of Paula, she knew how important the *T* in *STARRR* was because *T* stood for "Tell the Truth" to get better together, and that's what Paula had done when she told Ruth why she was resigning. Paula told the truth, and while it was hard to hear, she was correct, Ruth thought. *I just need to find a way for us as a team to tell the truth before people decide to make drastic changes like resigning.*

She looked at her notes on the page and the rest of the letters in *STARRR* and thought about what they stood for. *I'll share the rest with Paula and the team soon,* she thought. *We'll use it to turn things around, and I believe it is not too late.*

Tiles of Talent: Embracing Hybrid Team Trust

The Conversation

Ruth was ready when Paula arrived for their afternoon meeting. She had her notes in front of her and was ready to listen.

Ruth came out from behind her desk and asked Paula to sit at the small table in the corner of the room by the window and whiteboard. This part of her office was intended for collaboration, and Ruth wanted Paula to be able to see all of her body language while they spoke, and not be separated by a desk.

Ruth asked Paula if it was okay if she started, and Paula indicated that was fine.

Just as they were about to begin, Mitch and some of the rest of the team knocked on Ruth's office door and walked in one by one.

The entire executive team was in the office. All eight members of the BBDI executive team were usually only together for the Wednesday morning meetings. This was extremely unusual, but the last two days had been filled with surprises.

Mitch started by saying, "I think we should all talk."

The other vice presidents nodded their heads in agreement.

Ruth was not sure what to do, but she could see the words she wrote in her leather journal jumping into her mind's eye.

She knew this was the time for the light to shine and help her see the truth behind the current issues with her team. She cared about them. She cared about the company. She wanted to do the best for everyone involved.

"That sounds like a good idea, Mitch," said Ruth. She continued, "Thank you, everyone, for coming together to have a conversation. Let's pull enough chairs into the room, so we can all sit together."

Once they had enough chairs, they all arranged them in a circle.

Mitch said, "I wasn't planning on breaking my word to you, Ruth, but this morning I got a resignation from someone on my team, and it worried me. I went to talk to Melissa about it, and she revealed to me that she had a resignation on her team and had been thinking about leaving, too."

Melissa was the incredibly talented general counsel for the organization. She sat looking at Ruth with a genuinely sad look on her face.

"We care about you and the company and wanted to come have a difficult conversation," said Mitch.

He continued, "Lately all we've done is update our to-do lists and check the boxes of what you tell us the board wants. We have lost sight of our shared vision and greater purpose to create a world that relies on truth to make better decisions. We have not been talking about this together or with the people who report to us. Our culture has suffered, and we stopped making time to tell the truth and focus on what matters most—our relationships. We need to have regular conversations together and truly tell each other the truth as a team."

Ruth was surprised for a third time. She could not believe what she was hearing from Mitch. All the realizations from the last 48 hours were coming out in a team conversation that was long overdue. Even Paula looked relieved.

"First, I want to say I'm sorry," said Ruth as she nodded her head and her eyes brimmed with tears. "Second, I want to say thank you all for caring enough to tell me the truth. You are right. I needed to hear the truth you and Paula shared with me and what you are sharing now. We needed to talk to each other truthfully in our meetings and make time for our work and personal relationships. I know it will take some time, but I want to ask you for one more chance."

Ruth held up her leather journal and showed it to the group. "I believe these letters and model can save our company and help us achieve our mission," she explained. "Starting with us, especially me, having small egos and a big mission. Unfortunately, I got a big ego with all the pressure and expectations from the board, and the mission in my mind became smaller and smaller. I apologize and hope you can forgive me. The *T* in *STARRR* is 'Tell the Truth,' as Mitch just did at the perfect time. The fact that this is all happening now is not an accident and we can't get better individually and as a team if we don't tell the truth. And when we are telling the truth and having these kinds of conversations, we need to implement the *A* in *STARRR* and 'Assume Positive Intent.' Let's not ignore each other and assume the worst. Let's challenge each other and assume the best. Let's not take things personally. Let's assume that each person has the team and each other's best interest at heart," Ruth declared.

"I can see that's why you are all here right now," she continued, "and again I'm so sorry for all I have done wrong to bring us to this moment. But I know you have made me better and I vow to be a better leader and team-mate to you all going forward."

Ruth stood up, walked over to Paula, put her hand on her shoulder, and asked her, "Will you please stay and finish what we started? I don't want to do this without you."

She then looked at Mitch and said, "You don't have to leave, either. I'll make it so you don't have to choose work over your family. You can do both and we will make it work together. What do you say?" she asked in a tone that was only expecting a yes. "Will you stay so we can finish the mission together?"

Mitch and Paula looked at each other and then at Ruth. They didn't really want to leave. The past few months they felt Ruth was giving them no choice but to leave, but now because of Ruth's honesty, vulnerability, and commitment they felt like staying was the only choice. They nodded and said, "Yes, we will stay."

Ruth let out a big sigh of relief. "Thank you. Thank you," she said in a raised voice, realizing the significance of the moment and their decision. "I'm excited, team!" she shouted, clenching her fist and pumping it into the air as everyone smiled.

She took a deep breath, looked at Melissa, and said, "I'm happy to hear your concerns as well, and whatever they are, we can work through them." She looked around at everyone in the room. "I get it. I hear you. Things are going to be very different going forward."

Ruth held up her journal again and announced, "This is what you can expect from me. We are going to use this model to meet as a team first thing tomorrow morning, and we are going to implement the first *R* to create specific 'Rules of Engagement' to make sure we continue to have the necessary conversations for us to grow stronger together. For today, I want you go home or stay here, whatever works best for you, and let's get this product launch in gear. Tomorrow let's meet again for a new conversation and a fresh start. You can all still tell me if I do not hit the mark in the coming weeks, and of course you are free to still leave in the end. But I believe the best is yet to come and would like ninety days to show you. And I promise to give you the flexibility and trust you need to do your work wherever you deem appropriate for your personal and team's success."

Everyone was smiling. They still looked cautious, and Ruth was not sure Mitch and Paula would ultimately decide to stay after the excitement of the meeting wore off, but she felt she had an opportunity to transform the situation with the team and company, as well as her family and the loved ones of everyone on the executive team and throughout the company.

As the team left her office, she asked them not to have any more meetings that day. They would wait until tomorrow and continue to discuss everything together while sharing the truth as a team. No agendas. No secrets. Just the truth everyone needed to hear to get better, including her. As the last person exited her office, she looked down at her leather journal and started planning for tomorrow's meeting.

Deal with the Elephants

That night, while watching her college teammate's daughter's volleyball game on TV with her family, she recalled the time her coach put a small statue of an elephant on her desk. The coach told the team they were not going to have any elephants sabotage the team. The team had no idea what elephants had to do with a volleyball team, so he explained that elephants were a metaphor for unaddressed issues or team dynamics that could and would sabotage the team if they weren't dealt with. Elephants might include teammates not meeting the expectations of the other team members, selfishness, big egos, past disagreements that haven't been resolved, and a variety of other challenges that can divide a team. Whenever a player walked into the coach's office, she saw the small elephant statue on the desk, and it was a reminder they were going to deal with the elephants and address unresolved issues as a team. The coach also brought the elephant to practices and would ask the team to sit down and talk together. Ruth realized it was one of the reasons why they won several championships. She was thankful for this blast from the past, a positive memory that gave her a great idea of what to bring to her team meeting tomorrow.

On the way to the office Ruth stopped at one of those stores that sells just about everything and found exactly what she was looking for. It wasn't the perfect elephant, but for now it was good enough. It would symbolize the fact that from now on her team was going to be brutally and positively honest with one another and address all the issues that were keeping them from being their best.

The Meeting

When Ruth walked into the conference room she was surprised and thankful to see the entire team sitting there. Although she would have been fine if some had connected online, it encouraged her that they all thought it was important enough to be there in person. She knew that meeting virtually certainly had its benefits and, when done right by engaging people, could be useful and productive. But, she believed that in-person meetings had the power to create more connection.

Ruth sat down and put the small statue of the elephant on the table in front of her. Some team members laughed, and others smiled as Ruth said, "Team, from now on we are going to deal with the elephants in the room and on our team and in our company. We are going to address issues and have conversations like we are having today much more frequently. Difficult conversations don't have to be difficult." Then she stood up and grabbed a marker and wrote on the whiteboard, "Truth, Trust, Time, and Transformation.

Ruth continued, "The more we have conversations like this and implement the model I'm going to fully share with you right now, the better we will get at these conversations. The more we speak truth, the more it will lead to trust. The more we build trust over time, we will get stronger and better as a team, and that will lead to the transformation we want to see." Next, she expressed encouragement and genuine gratitude for each person and their contribution to the shared vision and greater purpose of BBDI. She invited them all to stay and be a part of the future together.

"And speaking of the future, it starts now," Ruth declared as she wrote *STARRR* on the whiteboard. "So let's start dealing with some elephants. Who wants to go first?" she asked the group. "What's an unresolved issue that we need to address, so it's no longer a roadblock? I know yesterday we talked about the roadblocks and issues I've created, and as you see, it's already making us better, but what else do we need to address?"

Thomas stood up. "Thanks for giving us the opportunity to speak, Ruth. I've been holding this in for a while. As the Chief Technology Officer of a company launching a new product, I find it quite stressful, and the fact that marketing is promising more than we can deliver really irritates me." Raising his voice louder with each word, he pointed to David, who was head of marketing, and added, "And I don't appreciate you always reminding me of the deadlines as if I don't already have it written on my whiteboard, computer, and even my freaking forehead. So give it a rest."

David shrugged awkwardly and looked around the room at all his teammates, who were looking at him wondering how he was going to respond. He stood up and shouted, "That's what we do in software, Thomas. We promise more and then we go to work to live up to the promise. That's how Microsoft and Apple became billion-dollar companies. And it's why I keep asking you about the deadline. It's not to be annoying. It's because I've been telling the industry and marketplace what's coming, and my reputation and all of our reputations are on the line! I won't ask again, and now that we will be having more relevant meetings I won't have to."

As the room became silent, Ruth thought to herself, *Wow, that escalated quickly.* She knew she had to fill the void, so she stood up and started clapping. "Okay, we are definitely having a much-needed conversation here. I'm glad we're airing out our concerns, but this is also a great opportunity to share the first *R* in the STARRR model and it's 'Rules of Engagement.' When having difficult conversations, we can make them less difficult by having Rules of Engagement on how to have these conversations. For example, I believe a key rule we need to implement is to avoid getting emotionally charged. We need to stay calm and civil when sharing truth and addressing issues."

David raised his hand and declared, "I vote for that." Everyone in the room laughed, except Thomas, who was still visibly upset.

Ruth addressed Thomas. "I know you're upset and I'm not saying you shouldn't share your concerns or frustration with how marketing is handling their business and questioning you on deadlines. We will come to an agreement on how best to handle marketing and product expectations. But when we have conversations like this in the future, I want you to share your concerns without getting emotionally charged. You share your concern; David responds. Then we talk it out to work it out. That's a great example of a Rule of Engagement, and now is a great time to talk about others we should implement. Anyone have another good one?"

Melissa raised her hand. "I propose a rule that says, 'No Meetings after the Meetings.' Too often at team meetings no one says anything, and then afterward we have all these smaller meetings where we comment about things we liked and disliked about what was said at the meeting. This means people don't know how to speak up succinctly about their ideas, or they are too afraid to speak up. Whatever the reason, this leads to division, not unity. If you're going to talk about it, then talk about it in the meeting and speak truth like Mitch and Ruth have said. Say it in the meeting or don't say it at all. Meetings after the meetings make it feel like we're a bunch of gossipers back in high school. It does not represent the culture or values of the organization or the type of leadership we want to provide to others in the company. The only meetings we should have after the meeting are to discuss the action items from the meeting and how to work together to make them happen."

"I like that rule," said Ruth, "Anyone disagree?" No one raised their hand.

"Everyone agree this should be a Rule of Engagement that we implement?" Everyone raised their hands.

"Great," she said. "Let's come up with a few more rules. We can always add more as issues come up."

Paula raised her hand next. "I have two. First, I think we should agree not to text or email when discussing sensitive topics. We should have these conversations in person or some way of seeing each other face-to-face, so words and intentions are not misconstrued, which often happens via email and text."

"How do you all feel about that?" Ruth asked. Everyone nodded in agreement.

"Okay great," said Ruth. "What else do you have?"

Paula continued, "I also don't think we should call our conversations difficult. Why do we have to put a negative label on it? How about we call them important or growth conversations or trust-building conversations? Or even business conversations? If we see these conversations as a positive, we'll look forward to having them instead of dreading them. These conversations are a natural part of business and life."

"Great idea," said David. "As we say in marketing, it's always about the story we're telling and what our audience is hearing that matters most." As a former actor turned Chief Marketing Officer, David loved talking about stories and perspectives. Turning a negative label to a positive one was always a good idea in his mind. He understood the power of managing your mindset and perspective, too, and was always ready to help others in this area as well.

"I agree," said Thomas, who was no longer shaking with frustration. "I want to apologize for getting emotionally charged and pointing at you, David, but the truth is these conversations aren't easy. So whatever we call them, we need to recognize that at times they might be difficult. I mean, you can come to my house and say the stainless steel door isn't stainless steel, but the door *is* stainless steel, whatever you want to think."

"I know what you mean," David responded, "But even though these conversations might be difficult, by implementing Ruth's model and looking at them as a positive, not a negative, they'll become less difficult. After all, these conversations are a necessity, and our mindset about them matters."

Thomas moved uncomfortably in his chair. David was creative, but Thomas was more logical. It's why they almost never agreed on anything. They just didn't see things the same way. "Well, we will just have to agree to disagree, as usual," he said.

Ruth intervened. "And sometimes that's the way it's going to be. We won't always agree. Or in Thomas and David's case, we may never agree. But the key is that we have this growth conversation, talk about and debate it, and when we make a decision—or I make a decision, because as the leader sometimes I have to decide what I think is best—then we all move forward in alignment and agreement. And during our conversations let's make sure we utilize the second *R* in the STARRR model and maintain 'Respect' for each other even when we disagree. Let's respect each other's opinions even if we don't have the same perspective or opinion. In this case, Thomas and David clearly disagree about what to call these conversations. I personally like calling them 'growth and trust-building conversations,' but I understand Thomas has a different perspective. He has a certain mindset that makes him a great CTO, but we wouldn't want him to be our head of marketing."

Everyone in the room laughed, then Ruth continued. "David has a perspective and mindset that makes him the best in the industry, but he would be a horrible CTO. So let's consider each other's perspectives and respect each other and each other's ideas when having our conversations. We won't always agree but we can respect each other even when we disagree. Our respect can be fueled by the fact that disagreement is actually a strength. We need to know how to manage it as a team."

"It's all about the relationship," Mitch added. "Without respect, you can't have great relationships, and if you don't have great relationships, you can't be a great team."

"I'm glad you said that," Ruth responded. "That's the last *R* in the STARRR model, and it's so important. Let's never lose sight of the fact that relationships mean everything. Let's not let disagreements or these conversations ruin our relationships. I lost sight of the importance of my relationship with you all and the relationships you have with each other, and it's why we experienced a downward spiral. I see it so clearly now, and again I have you all to thank."

Paula interjected, "I appreciate you saying that, Ruth, and agree a hundred percent, but in the spirit of transparency and truth I have to say something that is difficult, or I should say is hopefully growth-producing. It's that, while I appreciate what you're saying about your relationship with us, I think the biggest elephant we are ignoring is your relationship with the board and the pressure they're putting on you that affects your relationship with us. It's something that needs to be addressed, and I just want you to know that I have your back with however you are going to deal with the situation. Because at the end of the day we can all be aligned, but if the board is not aligned with us, then we're going to experience a titanic crash."

"I have your back, too," said Mitch.

"Me, too," said David.

"I'm all in," declared Melissa.

"Whatever you need from me, just say the word," added Thomas.

The rest of the team shared their support as a single tear of relief slipped down Ruth's face. She knew Paula was right. She looked at the elephant on the desk in front of her and knew her relationship with the board was strained and headed toward being broken if she didn't deal with this gigantic elephant. She knew they meant well and were incredible assets to the company. However, there was an opportunity to improve the dynamic that would help everyone.

"You are one hundred percent correct, Paula. Wow. Thank you for speaking the hard truth like that. It's painful but true. And thank you all for your support. I'm so glad we're on this team together. Let's break for the day and go attack our to-do list for this product launch. I know what I need to do. I need to go have a difficult—or I should say trust-building—conversation with the board. Everything we're working toward will depend on that."

Difficult Conversations Don't Have to be Difficult

Be Great Together

After the meeting, the team worked together to accomplish more in one day than they had in previous weeks. Ruth called the board to schedule an emergency meeting for the next day. She felt excited about her team's unity and progress, while also dreading the meeting with the board. She knew she should not dread the opportunity to change the dynamic with the board and worked to shift her mindset the way she had done with her team. As she sat on her couch at home with a notebook and pen preparing for the meeting, she thought about what points she should make and possible scenarios of how the meeting would go. She realized she hadn't been speaking truth to the board, and that was her fault, not theirs. Ruth wanted to take the time to prepare and communicate in a way that would be a big win for everyone as an example of a growth conversation.

Her husband and family were out at her youngest son's basketball game, and she had told them earlier in the evening that she would be starting to come to more games again. Ruth knew she had to create great relationships at home and at work to perform well in either environment and have joy in the process. She knew it wasn't easy for any home or business leader, but that it could be done by putting relationships first. It's something the board needs to do as well, instead of the passive-aggressive and ego-centric meetings they were having.

She realized that, at the end of the day, she had to be bold and take a stand for herself and her team and the mission they were truly trying to accomplish. She would need to be clear and firm, because the board would not respond well to a lack of clarity. She always did things her way, what she believed was the right way, and now was not the time to play defense or act scared.

Ruth looked at the STARRR model she had scribbled in her notes and realized she should call it the STAR³ model. It was easier to say and explain, and honestly felt hipper and more unique. She thought of the last two *R*s, Respect and Relationships, and remembered reading a story about Kerri Walsh Jennings and Misty May-Treanor, who made up the greatest beach volleyball duo of all time. They were a legendary team who won a number of championships. They sometimes had disagreements but they always respected each other and remembered relationship and their teamwork were what mattered most. They said they wanted to be great together, and this is what made them great. They weren't going to let trivial things or disagreements get in their way of being great together. They had small egos and a big mission and embodied the STAR³ model. This gave Ruth an idea of what she needed to do and say at her meeting tomorrow. She and the board had to become a united team that wanted to be great together. Otherwise, the board would have to find a new leader and she would find a new company to lead. Yes, she and the board were going to have a very uncomfortable but growth-producing conversation.

The Board Meeting

On her way into the office, Ruth stopped to give T a fist-bump like she had each day since their first meeting. It had become their ritual and for Ruth it served as a reminder to stay strong and continue to speak truth and build trust in order to see transformation over time.

"I have a big elephant to deal with today," Ruth told T.

"You've got this," T responded. "If anyone can do it, it's you, and I know you've got this."

"We'll see," said Ruth as she carried a big bag into the office along with her laptop. As she walked toward the conference room to meet the board, her nerves told her this was a big moment. She believed that every moment mattered and yet she found there were certain moments that were bigger than others, and this was certainly going to be one of those defining moments in her life. Ruth took a deep breath and exhaled slowly. She continued to visualize a successful meeting and knew the conversations they were going to have and the object lesson she was about to share could produce powerful results.

When she walked into the conference room, some of the board members were already there. After putting the big bag and laptop by her seat, she walked over to them and thanked them for coming on such short notice. After all the board members had arrived and taken their seats, Ruth began the meeting by thanking them for coming.

"I know you're probably wondering why I asked to have this emergency meeting," Ruth began, "but before

I go into that I want to do a little exercise with you." The look on their faces told Ruth this was the last thing they wanted to do, but she told herself to be bold and that it was okay to make them uncomfortable.

Ruth pulled a bunch of volleyballs out of her big bag and threw them to the different board members sitting around the table. She could tell they were confused, irritated, and all of them were wondering what this had to do with any business emergency they were meeting about. In a strong, commanding voice, she instructed them, "Those of you with a ball, I want you to hit the ball in the air using your two hands like this." She demonstrated the way a setter would hit the ball for a teammate to spike it and hit it nice and easy toward a board member without a ball. "Then, if a ball comes your way, I want you to do the same thing with two hands and gently hit it to guide it toward another person in the room. Let's see how long we can keep the balls in the air. And please pay attention. We don't want any bruised noses." Then she shouted in a tone that gave them no option to opt out of the exercise, "Ready, go!"

To their credit, the board members gave her the benefit of the doubt and started to hit the balls toward each other. Within a few seconds all the balls were on the ground. As she suspected, they were much better at business than at sports. One of the board members who was clearly annoyed and frustrated asked, "What was the point of that?"

Ruth responded, "I'm about to show you if you give me a few more minutes." She asked one of the board members, James, to join her in the most spacious part of the room and stand a few feet away from her. She picked up a ball and hit it to him. He hit it back to her, and they did this ten times before she grabbed the ball and sat back down in her chair and instructed James to do the same.

"Now let's all do this together with just one ball," she said in an encouraging tone." This time the group was able to keep the ball in the air for about 30 seconds before Marlo missed it and the ball hit the wall and then the floor. "Okay, we need to work on our hitting, Marlo, but overall, great job, team. You asked the point of this, and I wanted to show you what it looks like when we are focusing on a bunch of balls in the air and don't have the skill or teamwork to manage them all. Then I wanted to show you what it looks like when two teammates work together and focus on one objective and what it looks like when an entire team works together to focus on one thing. Sure, we dropped the ball after about half a minute, but imagine if we kept working on this together. We'd continue to get better and find a way to keep the ball in the air for as long as we wanted to. This is the power of focusing on one thing as a united team. I asked you all here today because we are not focused on one thing—we have a lot of balls in the air and as a board we are not united and are not working together as a team. Like our first try with all the balls at once, all our goals and plans for success will crash to the ground if we don't make some changes now!"

Ruth knew she had made her point and had their attention, but she also expected resistance and questions. To no one's surprise, James said, "But the new product launch is not going well, and whose fault is it that we have all these balls in the air? You are the leader of this company."

"You are right, James. I am the leader. And I take full responsibility. I was more worried about meeting the board's expectations—which quite frankly varies depending on which board member I'm talking to—and this has caused more balls to fly through the air. I've allowed it to distract me from leading my team and from focusing on the mission of this great company."

"So what do you plan do to about it?" Marlo asked as she picked up the ball that had fallen to the ground.

"I've already started to do something about it," Ruth said. "I've had a few great meetings with my team, and yesterday we accomplished more in one day than we had in the previous weeks. And that's why I knew we all had to meet. My team and I are now aligned, and we need all of us to be aligned if we are going to be successful. We can't have five balls in the air. We all have to agree on what expectations we are striving to meet, what goal we are working toward, and develop great relationships as we live and share our one mission. We have to have oneness of mission, focus, and execution. Let's pick one ball and focus on that and win together."

"How do you suggest we do this?" asked James.

"I'm glad you asked," Ruth said as she went to the whiteboard and wrote "STAR³" on it. "We used this model to have growth conversations as a team. I believe we can use it right now to help us get aligned and focused."

Ruth proceeded to explain the model to them. When it came to the part about Relationships, she said, "My relationships with my team are a priority and our relationships as a board need to be a priority. If we can have these necessary conversations, work through our disagreements, and come to a consensus on how we move forward, there will be no stopping us. While we all want to sell the company, I've realized that it can't be my goal. Our goal must be to develop great relationships and become a great team that works together to achieve our mission and create a successful product launch. If we do that, the sale will be a byproduct of what we achieve together. As my sister Mary always says, 'If you want the fruit, you need to focus on the root.'"

James nodded. "I couldn't agree more. So let's take as long as we need to have the conversation."

And that's what they did all morning, and past noon. Ruth took them through the STAR³ model as they told the truth, disagreed, fought, cleared the air, calmed down, and created the Rules of Engagement for the board and a focused plan for the next 90 days. They agreed to have more difficult (growth and truthful) conversations as a board and not to let egos, divisiveness, and distractions keep them from their goals. As they left the meeting, they thanked Ruth for her leadership and the helpful new model they were going to take back to their own companies and teams.

When the last board member left, Ruth let out a sigh of relief as she grabbed a ball and spiked it against the floor. She felt a thousand pounds lighter and more confident than ever about the board, her team, and the company's future. She would have to have more conversations with both her board and her team, but now she had a powerful and practical way to turn struggle into strength and frustration into focus. There was just one piece missing from her team and she knew exactly what she had to do next.

The T-urnaround

Meeting with her team the next day in the conference room, Ruth shared details about the successful meeting with the board and the alignment that was created. Her excitement and enthusiasm were contagious, and her team beamed with hope and optimism about their future. After debriefing them about the board and the 90-day plan, she revisited the debate Thomas and David had about over-promising on a product that wasn't ready yet. She wanted her team to know that when issues arose, they could count on her to bring disagreements to a resolution in order to provide closure and clarity.

"I understand the different perspectives that Thomas and David have," she told them. "And here's the deal. In technology, if you aren't promising something you're still in the process of creating, then you wouldn't have anything new to sell. We've all heard of prototypes and pilots, right? While that situation is stressful, we will always be promoting and promising our new offerings, and then we'll have to work like heck to turn a prototype into reality. It's the nature of this industry and business. We sell. We promise. We create. We deliver. We just have to make sure we work together and support each other to meet our deadlines. So, are we good with this? Can we move on?" she asked the team.

Everyone said yes, even Thomas, who realized that the stress had gotten the best of him.

"Great," said Ruth. "Now I have a surprise for you. It's something I've been thinking a lot about as we get ready to create an amazing turnaround." Ruth walked over to the conference room door and opened it. On the other side was T. She was smiling. She accepted Ruth's extended hand and shook it, then walked into the conference room. Everyone knew T. She had helped protect each of them in her own special way over the past six years.

Ruth continued, "*Turnaround* starts with *T* and our T is going to help us turn this ship around. I've asked her to join our company as the Chief Security Officer and serve as our Chief Trust Officer for our ongoing meetings and conversations. I would like her to help us maintain a focus on our relationships, building trust, and keeping us accountable in telling each other the truth. She did this for me, and I know she will help us all stay on the right track."

Everyone on the team smiled. It was a surprising but obvious choice. T had had one-on-one conversations with

65

all of the team members. They all trusted her and felt she would help them continue to build trust with each other. They also knew she was very protective, had excellent discretion, and would be diligent about protecting them and their new technology.

"So let's give T a hand and welcome her to the team," said Ruth. Everyone clapped and cheered as T smiled and walked around the room thanking everyone. "I can't thank you enough," she said to Ruth. "I'm excited about this opportunity to work with you all and I will do my best to continue to help you improve and grow."

"We are thankful to have you on the team. And we will need *all* of you to achieve our goals in the next ninety days," said Ruth as she pointed to each member of the team. "It's going to take a lot of work and a lot of conversations to make it happen, so let's remember to live the STAR^3 model," she said as she wrote "STAR^3" on the board. Then she wrote "MISSION" in big letters next to it. "And let's remember our mission as we move forward. With small egos, let's focus on our big mission. In every difficult and growth conversation, we should always remind ourselves and each other of our mission. Our conversations should serve to make us stronger as we strive to live and share our mission."

Then she did the volleyball exercise with her leadership team as she had done with the board. With many former athletes on her leadership team, the group was definitely more skilled on their first try than the board, but the lesson and response was the same. And they didn't need to be athletes to know the message was clear. Focus on one thing. Keep their eyes on the prize. This was the mission: accomplishing something impactful together as a team, not the sale of the company. Work together. Grow stronger together using the STAR^3 model.

Ruth closed out the meeting by telling them, "Dominate the day." She knew it was going to be a great one.

Chapter 6

Time to Transform

In the weeks that followed, Ruth kept her commitments to the team, and the team kept their commitments to each other. Commitment recognizes commitment, and this led to enhanced trust and the team genuinely caring about each other. They were no longer fighting against each other. Now they were fighting *for* each other. They had many conversations and meetings along the way and the STAR³ model helped increase their respect and appreciation for each other. They still fought and disagreed, but because they had trust and respect, the fighting made them stronger rather than weaker. It made them closer instead of tearing them apart. They operated like an elite executive team that knows what it takes to be the best in the world.

Along the way, Ruth realized that fighting wasn't the problem on a team. The lack of trust and respect was what caused the demise. Families fight. But if they have love and respect and they fight fairly with the right rules of engagement, this leads to greater connection and commitment. Ruth saw firsthand her dysfunctional team transformed into a focused family. Whether or not they sold the company mattered far less to Ruth. Seeing her team become a real team was one of the greatest rewards of her life. She loved how they started each meeting by stating their shared vision and greater purpose and told each other the truth respectfully in their ongoing conversations.

She got fired up anytime someone would offer a new Rule of Engagement to make their conversations better and more productive. She high-fived team members when they challenged her and made her build a case for why she made certain decisions. She got great joy seeing friendships blossom—even between David and Thomas—and most of all she was pleasantly surprised when the team decided to work in the office Monday through Thursday and from home on Friday. She didn't force it. They brought the idea to her, and she said she supported whatever the team decided was best. And she loved seeing T thrive in her role with the company and leadership team. She did exactly what Ruth hoped she would do and served as the glue that made the team better.

Chapter 7

Team

Over time, the team's relationships and trust grew stronger and so did their bonds. The thought of leaving the company was no longer a question. Everyone stayed through the product launch, which occurred on the 80th day after Ruth's defining meeting with the board.

It was a huge success in the marketplace and everyone in the industry took notice. The board was beyond ecstatic. The team felt an immense amount of pride in their accomplishment. Ruth was thankful for everything and everyone that had brought her to this moment.

On the 90th day she celebrated with her team at her favorite restaurant, which she rented out for the occasion.

On the 111th day BBDI sold for almost twice the board's target sale price. It wasn't a decision she made alone. Of course, the board advocated for the sale of the company, but so did the leadership team. Ruth told them she wouldn't sell the company without their blessing, and they all supported her decision to accept an offer that was too good to refuse.

On the day of the sale, Ruth was not as happy as she thought she would be. She had conflicting emotions. She had achieved a professional feat and a financial victory most people only dream of, and yet she was sad that it meant the journey with her team was over. It's a strange feeling to get everything you've ever wanted and not be satisfied, she thought. She knew there was something else she needed to do but wasn't quite sure what it was.

An emptiness stayed with her even while celebrating on a much-deserved trip to Italy with her family. It was their first true family vacation in a decade and while she loved eating fresh pasta and creamy gelato with her husband and four children, she knew something was missing. While seeing a group of business-people meeting at a local café, she received a clear glimpse of what it was.

One More Meeting

Upon returning from her trip to Italy, Ruth invited her leadership team over to her house. The terms of the sale of the company did not require her to stay on as the CEO. She felt it was best to step aside and knew she needed a break. Most of her team also decided to leave as well, with generous payouts they received from the sale. New leadership was coming in, and it made sense for the current team to transition. Ruth didn't have to work again, but they did, and so they were curious to hear why Ruth wanted to meet with them. Many of them had become rock stars in the industry and had received incredible offers and opportunities to be a part of other top companies looking to build greater success.

After engaging in small-talk and reminiscing about the previous six months and the incredible turnaround, Ruth began, "I know you're probably wondering why I invited you all here today. Of course, I love you all and you are family who is welcome over anytime, but obviously I didn't invite you today to just have a nice lunch and chitchat. I invited you because we need to have one more STAR^3 conversation and the topic is starting a new company together. I'm not done with you or this team. And I hope you aren't done with me. I feel like we're just getting started. There is so much we can do and build together, and our team can truly continue to change the world in meaningful ways."

Ruth surveyed the room and looked into her team's eyes to see if they were as excited about this as she was. She continued, "What am I going to do, hang out with my family and travel the world for the rest of my life? Of course not. My family knows how much you all mean to me, and they can't imagine life without us building something special together. Our families have walked through this journey together. I want to do this, and I hope you do, too. Of course, I'll make it worth your while financially, and every one of you will get equity in our new venture, making you significant owners of the company that will create generational wealth for all our loved ones. But just as we turned around BBDI, we will create success by focusing on a new mission, not on the money. So, what do you say?" Ruth finished, clapping her hands before pumping her fists.

Paula was the first team member to speak up. "The fact that you want to do this with us again when you don't have to means a lot. I know all our families and loved ones will appreciate this, too. All the company picnics, long work hours, and ups and downs through the years were worth it! We have more great work to do together, and now we've learned so much about being a great team, we will have more exciting products to create for the world."

"I appreciate your desire to make another run with us," said Mitch. "I agree we were just getting started before we sold and I'm excited to see what we can build next."

"I agree," said Thomas. "I'm ready to get to work again. The last few months were the most enjoyable time of my career. If we can bring this same teamwork approach to a new company, I'm all in."

"I love it. But what is it that we're going to build?" asked David. "What will our mission be? You know I need something to market and a story to tell before we have a product," he said, laughing out loud.

"That's a great question," answered Ruth. "And that's what I want this conversation to be about. I'm fired up you're ready to do this with me, so let's talk about what we want to create together using the STAR^3 model. With small egos, let's talk about our next big mission. Let's imagine a future that we can create together. And after we decide this, let's use the T4 action plan created for us by our own Chief Trust Officer, T, that will help us continue to speak truth, build trust, and create transformation over time. The four Ts are powerful: truth told as a team builds trust over time, which leads to transformation."

Ruth turned to T, who was sitting next to her. They fist-bumped, and Ruth thanked her for creating such a great action plan to complement the STAR^3 model. "We're just going to keep getting better," she exclaimed. "Okay, let's get started. What do you want to create next?"

After a few hours of telling the truth about what was in their hearts and respecting each other's ideas for what each person believed the world needed next, they ultimately decided they wanted to create a new technology product that would strengthen and protect relationships. Maybe it would be something in the field of cybersecurity. They weren't exactly sure what they would create next, but they had their mission. They had their STAR^3 model. They had the framework for their T4 action plan. They had each other, and they were ready to create a new company and future together.

Chapter 8

Application of the STAR³ Model

Difficult Conversations Don't Have to be Difficult Recap

One of the most powerful things for team trust and performance is to have the difficult conversations.

Teams must have the significant conversations, but in a positive way. It will not always be easy but if you do this as a team, the conversations will get easier, especially with the STAR³ model and your own Rules of Engagement.

The truth is, having conversations that are hard can be hard. We do get nervous and even scared to have some of the important conversations in our life and work. However, difficult conversations really do not have to be difficult. Exceptional leaders and teams understand this truth and work to get better at addressing any issue or topic. Just like anything else, you have to study and practice to get better. The reason these conversations represent such a massive opportunity is because most people we talk to avoid them or hope someone else will deal with the issue. People also tell us in our consulting work, "I was hoping it would go away or resolve itself somehow." What we've found is that the teams who practice the discipline and commitment to have the more challenging and tough conversations actually grow. The teams and individuals get stronger. They learn how to appreciate other points of view, and then the performance improves, too. You have to be patient. You have to use the elements of the STAR³ model, and you have to trust the process. When you practice and work together to get better, trust will grow, and so will everyone on the team. The STAR^3 model and a T4 action plan can give you the structure to succeed.

STEP 1

Teams should review the model together and create your own rules of engagement that are specific to your team or organization. Next, you'll customize your T4 action plan to tell the truth and transform over time.

STEP 2

Complete a T4 action plan together.

T1: Be transparent with each other. Ask each team member: Where would you like to see more transparency on the team?

T2: Be truthful with each other and yourself. Talk about how often you tell the truth to each other as a team. Where could greater truth be helpful? How can you support each other more in telling the truth to get better together?

T3: Believe in transformation. Ask each person on the team what type of transformation they would like to see (no matter how seemingly small).

T4: Transformation takes time, so invest the time. The entire team has to trust the process and understand that it will take time for people to get comfortable, transparent, trusting, and ultimately transform. The time it takes requires patience and grace for each person on the team.

STEP 3

Begin practicing the STAR^3 model as a team. Review the model on a weekly basis and before conversations that may present more challenging situations and topics.

STEP 4

Discuss and celebrate progress.

STEP 5

Update rules of engagement as needed.

The truth will help the team accomplish great things together. The truth will be a guiding force for an outstanding culture that includes excellence in leadership and teamwork. Your team and organization will grow individually and collectively.

STAR³

The Model: STAR³

S   Small ego/big mission. WE > Me

T   Tell the truth to get better together.

A   Assume positive intent. Do not take it personally. Manage emotional energy. No personal attacks.

R^1 Rules of Engagement. Create specific rules of engagement for your team when using the STAR³ model.

R^2 Respect your team and the process.

R^3 Relationships matter most.

Difficult Conversations Don't Have to be Difficult

Difficult Conversations Don't Have to be Difficult *Resources*

Visit www.difficultconversationsbook.com for:

- Action Plan for you and your team as you read *Difficult Conversations Don't Have to be Difficult*
- A T4 Action Plan Template to fill out with your team to move forward
- A downloadable copy of the STAR^3 model
- Workshops, Training, Coaching, Leadership Offsites, and Speaking for your team and organization

To have Jon or Amy speak to your company or organization about becoming a strong team contact The Jon Gordon Companies at:

Phone: 904-285-6842
Email: info@jongordon.com
Online: JonGordon.com
Twitter: @JonGordon11
Facebook: Facebook.com/JonGordonpage
Instagram: JonGordon11

Sign up for Jon's weekly positive tip at: JonGordon.com.

About the Authors

Jon Gordon has inspired millions of readers around the world. He is the author of 30 books, including five children's books and 15 bestsellers, among them *The Energy Bus, The Carpenter, Training Camp, You Win in the Locker Room First, The Power of Positive Leadership, The Power of a Positive Team, The Coffee Bean, Stay Positive, The Garden, Relationship Grit, Stick Together, Row the Boat,* and *The Sale.* He is passionate about developing positive leaders, organizations, and teams. Visit him at JonGordon.com.

Amy P. Kelly is a global human resources and talent development executive known for building high-performing talent and cultures, including award-winning workplaces and leadership development programs. Her passion is to help individuals become the leaders they were created to be. Amy believes in people and partners to build successful leaders and teams in all aspects of life, whether at home with her husband and four children, in her community, or in organizations around the word. Amy's other books include: *The Energy Bus*

Field Guide, G.L.U.E. A Leadership Development Strategy to Bond and Unite, You Grow Girl! Plant and Pursue the Power of You, and the *You Grow Girl! Journal.* For more information about Amy and her work, visit www.amypkelly.com.

Other Books by Jon Gordon

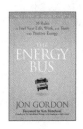

The Energy Bus

A man whose life and career are in shambles learns from a unique bus driver and set of passengers how to overcome adversity. Enjoy an enlightening ride of positive energy that is improving the way leaders lead, employees work, and teams function. **www.TheEnergyBus.com**

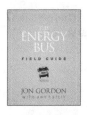

The Energy Bus Field Guide

Jon Gordon's international bestseller, *The Energy Bus,* has inspired thousands of businesses, organizations, sport teams, schools, and families alike, helping them cultivate positive energy, overcome adversity, and bring out the best in themselves and those around them. *The Energy Bus Field Guide* is a simple and powerful guide for putting *The Energy Bus* lessons to work. Using the 10 principles, you'll discover how to navigate the twists and turns that often sabotage individual and team success, and how to move in the right direction with vision, focus, purpose, and positive energy.

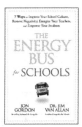

The Energy Bus for Schools

Based on *The Energy Bus*, the *Wall Street Journal* bestseller by lead author Jon Gordon, *The Energy Bus for Schools* teaches educators how to fuel their schools, themselves, and their students with positive energy. Research shows that culture and leadership greatly influence a school's learning environment and students' academic success. This book will help teachers work together to create a school culture where school leaders and students can grow into positive leaders, energizing their school culture as a united front.

The No Complaining Rule

Follow a vice president of human resources who must save herself and her company from ruin and discover proven principles and an actionable plan to win the battle against individual and organizational negativity.
www.NoComplainingRule.com

Training Camp

This inspirational story about a small guy with a big heart, and a special coach who guides him on a quest for excellence, reveals the 11 winning habits that separate the best individuals and teams from the rest.
www.TrainingCamp11.com

The Shark and the Goldfish

Delightfully illustrated, this quick read is packed with tips and strategies on how to respond to challenges beyond your control in order to thrive during waves of change.
www.SharkandGoldfish.com

Soup

The newly appointed CEO of a popular soup company is brought in to reinvigorate the brand and bring success back to a company that has fallen on hard times. Through her journey, discover the key ingredients to unite, engage, and inspire teams to create a culture of greatness.
www.Soup11.com

The Seed

Go on a quest for the meaning and passion behind work with Josh, an up-and-comer at his company who is disenchanted with his job. Through Josh's cross-country journey, you'll find surprising new sources of wisdom and inspiration in your own business and life.
www.Seed11.com

Other Books by Jon Gordon

One Word

One Word is a simple concept that delivers powerful life change! This quick read will inspire you to simplify your life and work by focusing on just one word for this year. *One Word* creates clarity, power, passion, and life-change. When you find your word, live it, and share it; your life will become more rewarding and exciting than ever.

www.getoneword.com

The Positive Dog

We all have two dogs inside of us. One dog is positive, happy, optimistic, and hopeful. The other dog is negative, mad, pessimistic, and fearful. These two dogs often fight inside us, but guess who wins? The one you feed the most. *The Positive Dog* is an inspiring story that not only reveals the strategies and benefits of being positive, but also an essential truth: being positive doesn't just make you better; it makes everyone around you better.

www.feedthepositivedog.com

The Carpenter

The Carpenter is Jon Gordon's most inspiring book yet—filled with powerful lessons and success strategies. Michael wakes up in the hospital with a bandage on his head and fear in his heart after collapsing during a morning jog. When Michael finds out the man who saved his life is a carpenter, he visits him and quickly learns that he is more than just a carpenter; he is also a builder of lives, careers, people, and teams. In this journey, you will learn timeless principles to help you stand out, excel, and make an impact on people and the world.

www.carpenter11.com

Other Books by Jon Gordon

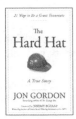

The Hard Hat

A true story about Cornell lacrosse player George Boiardi, *The Hard Hat* is an unforgettable book about a selfless, loyal, joyful, hard-working, competitive, and compassionate leader and teammate, the impact he had on his team and program, and the lessons we can learn from him. This inspirational story will teach you how to build a great team and be the best teammate you can be.
www.hardhat21.com

You Win in the Locker Room First

Based on the extraordinary experiences of NFL Coach Mike Smith and leadership expert Jon Gordon, *You Win in the Locker Room First* offers a rare, behind-the-scenes look at one of the most pressure-packed leadership jobs on the planet, and what leaders can learn from these experiences in order to build their own winning teams.
www.wininthelockerroom.com

Life Word

Life Word reveals a simple, powerful tool to help you identify the word that will inspire you to live your best life while leaving your greatest legacy. In the process, you'll discover your *why*, which will help show you how to live with a renewed sense of power, purpose, and passion.
www.getoneword.com/lifeword

The Power of Positive Leadership

The Power of Positive Leadership is your personal coach for becoming the leader your people deserve. Jon Gordon gathers insights from his bestselling fables to bring you the definitive guide to positive leadership. Difficult times call for leaders who are up to the challenge. Results are the by-product of your culture, teamwork, vision, talent, innovation, execution, and commitment. This book shows you how to bring it all together to become a powerfully positive leader.
www.powerofpositiveleadership.com

Other Books by Jon Gordon

The Power of a Positive Team

In *The Power of a Positive Team*, Jon Gordon draws on his unique team-building experience, as well as conversations with some of the greatest teams in history, to provide an essential framework of proven practices to empower teams to work together more effectively and achieve superior results.
www.PowerOfAPositiveTeam.com

The Coffee Bean

From bestselling author Jon Gordon and rising star Damon West comes *The Coffee Bean*: an illustrated fable that teaches readers how to transform their environment, overcome challenges, and create positive change.
www.coffeebeanbook.com

Stay Positive

Fuel yourself and others with positive energy—inspirational quotes and encouraging messages to live by from bestselling author, Jon Gordon. Keep this little book by your side, read from it each day, and feed your mind, body, and soul with the power of positivity.
www.StayPositiveBook.com

The Garden

The Garden is an enlightening and encouraging fable that helps readers overcome the 5 D's (doubt, distortion, discouragement, distractions, and division) in order to find more peace, focus, connection, and happiness. Jon tells a story of teenage twins who, through the help of a neighbor and his special garden, find ancient wisdom, life-changing lessons, and practical strategies to overcome the fear, anxiety, and stress in their lives.
www.readthegarden.com

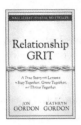

Relationship Grit

Bestselling author Jon Gordon is back with another life-affirming book. This time, he teams up with Kathryn Gordon, his wife of 23 years, for a look at what it takes to build strong relationships. In *Relationship Grit*, the Gordons reveal what brought them together, what kept them together through difficult times, and what continues to sustain their love and passion for one another to this day.

www.relationshipgritbook.com

Stick Together

From bestselling author Jon Gordon and coauthor Kate Leavell, *Stick Together* delivers a crucial message about the power of belief, ownership, connection, love, inclusion, consistency, and hope. The authors guide individuals and teams on an inspiring journey to show them how to persevere through challenges, overcome obstacles, and create success together.

www.sticktogetherbook.com

Row the Boat

In *Row the Boat*, Minnesota Golden Gophers Head Coach P.J. Fleck and bestselling author Jon Gordon deliver an inspiring message about what you can achieve when you approach life with a never-give-up philosophy. The book shows you how to choose enthusiasm and optimism as your guiding lights instead of being defined by circumstances and events outside of your control.

www.rowtheboatbook.com

The Sale

In *The Sale*, bestselling author Jon Gordon and rising star Alex Demczak deliver an invaluable lesson about what matters most in life and work and how to achieve it. The book teaches four lessons about integrity in order to create lasting success.

www.thesalebook.com

Other Books by Jon Gordon

The One Word Journal

In *The One Word Journal*, bestselling authors Jon Gordon, Dan Britton, and Jimmy Page deliver a powerful new approach to simplifying and transforming your life and business. You'll learn how to access the core of your intention every week of the year as you explore 52 weekly lessons, principles, and wins that unleash the power of your One Word.

How to Be a Coffee Bean

In *How to Be a Coffee Bean*, bestselling coauthors of *The Coffee Bean*, Jon Gordon and Damon West, present 111 simple and effective strategies to help you lead a coffee bean lifestyle— one full of healthy habits, encouragement, and genuine happiness. From athletes to students and executives, countless individuals have been inspired by *The Coffee Bean* message. Now, *How to Be a Coffee Bean* teaches you how to put *The Coffee Bean* philosophy into action to help you create real and lasting change in your life.

The One Truth

In *The One Truth*, bestselling author and thought leader Jon Gordon guides you on a path to discover revolutionary insights, ancient truths, and practical strategies to elevate your mind, unlock your power, and live life to the fullest. Once you know the One Truth, you'll see how it impacts leadership, teamwork, mindset, performance, relationships, addictions, social media, anxiety, mental health, healing, and ultimately determines what you create and experience.

The Energy Bus for Kids

The illustrated children's adaptation of the bestselling book *The Energy Bus* tells the story of George, who, with the help of his school bus driver, Joy, learns that if he believes in himself, he'll find the strength to overcome any challenge. His journey teaches kids how to overcome negativity, bullies, and everyday challenges to be their best.
www.EnergyBusKids.com

Other Books by Jon Gordon

Thank You and Good Night

Thank You and Good Night is a beautifully illustrated book that shares the heart of gratitude. Jon Gordon takes a little boy and girl on a fun-filled journey from one perfect moonlit night to the next. During their adventurous days and nights, the children explore the people, places, and things they are thankful for.

The Hard Hat for Kids

The Hard Hat for Kids is an illustrated guide to teamwork. Adapted from the bestseller *The Hard Hat*, this uplifting story presents practical insights and life-changing lessons that are immediately applicable to everyday situations, giving kids—and adults—a new outlook on cooperation, friendship, and the selfless nature of true teamwork.
www.HardHatforKids.com

One Word for Kids

If you could choose only one word to help you have your best year ever, what would it be? *Love? Fun? Believe? Brave?* It's probably different for each person. How you find your word is just as important as the word itself. And once you know your word, what do you do with it? In *One Word for Kids,* bestselling author Jon Gordon—along with coauthors Dan Britton and Jimmy Page—asks these questions to children and adults of all ages, teaching an important life lesson in the process.
www.getoneword.com/kids

The Coffee Bean for Kids

The bestselling authors of *The Coffee Bean* inspire and encourage children with this transformative tale of personal strength. Perfect for parents, teachers, and children who wish to overcome negativity and challenging situations, *The Coffee Bean for Kids* teaches readers about the potential that each one of us has to lead, influence, and make a positive impact on others and the world.
www.coffeebeankidsbook.com

Other Books by Jon Gordon